VAN HALEN

A VISUAL HISTORY: 1978 – 1984
BY NEIL ZLOZOWER

Foreword by David Lee Roth

CHRONICLE BOOKS

SAN FRANCISCO

Library of Congress Cataloging-in-Publication Data available.
ISBN: 978-0-8118-6304-9

Manufactured in China

Art Direction & Design: Tom Jermann / t42design
Copy Editor: Frank Meyer

10 9 8 7 6 5 4 3 2

Chronicle Books LLC
680 Second Street
San Francisco, California 94107
www.chroniclebooks.com

This is my very first published book and I would like to give special thanks to the following people:

Tom Jermann: Thanks for everything because without you and your vision, this book would have NEVER happened!

My mom and dad: Thanks for all the love, patience, guidance, knowledge, and wisdom!!!!

Zak Zlozower, the person in my life who keeps me going and is also the coolest guy in the world!

David Lee Roth, the greatest entertainer ever!!!!!

Plus,
Ruby
Michael Anthony
Steve Mockus and everyone at Chronicle Books!!!!
Peter Mallick – Thanks for everything as always!!!!
David Atlas – Thanks man!!!
Baret and Vic Lepejian
Rosa Gomez
The staff at A&I Photographic and Digital Services. The BEST photo lab / imaging house in the world!!!
Frank Meyer
Byrd Leavell – Man, we almost had it!!!!
Toby Yoo
Buddha
Dalai Lama
Nyree Bird – Thanks for all the help with "LIFE."
Illantra
Fidar
Evesta
Jes Christensen
Silvia Brown
Deepak Chopra
Zakk and Barbaranne Wylde – Love you guys!!!!!!!!!!!!!
Randall Rhoads
Jimi Hendrix
Matt Sencio
Michael Karlin
Bill Lonero
Sandy Martin Plute – Something special!!!!
Carmen Cole
Matt Beal "Awake"
Emmy Burns
Pete Angelus
Ted Templeman
Brad Tolinski

And all the Van Halen fans throughout the world, because without you guys,
there wouldn't have been this incredible band who made such INSANE music!!!!

THANKS!!!!!!
LOVE,

Zloz

Foreword

Looking at the pictures was always more fun than looking at the music.

Your ears are only the side door for truth. Our eyes tell the real story, and with "Zloz" it's a series of "a thousand word" photos that have come to speak even more volumes with time.

Neil's work routinely captures the artist's vision, however content-rich or content-free, and delights in the process. While the tunes freeze a moment of intangible passion, great photography tells a better story. More importantly, perhaps we as people become more available to the realities of who we were and what the hell was I thinking when I wore that?

Frequently the simple idea that you had the willingness to "wear something like that" qualified as your entire personal statement. And all the statements are here, as well as all the ambition, delusions, faith, dreams, and small but manageable drinking problems. I have often found that by the time my dreams come true, I've turned into somebody else. Zlozower's images remind us of who we were before that happened.

Neil is a rock star. His work will survive long after he puts down his camera. His efforts are internationally famous and you don't need to speak English to enjoy the show. His career is verging on Rolling Stones size and he is at home everywhere from Tokyo to Cheyenne.

How important is my great friend's contribution to the general proceedings? If you had to choose, which would you rather be, deaf or blind? That's what I thought. Me too.

Nothin' but love — Nothin' but yeah!

— David Lee Roth

Introduction

The year: 1978
The place: Hollywood, California

I was a twenty-four-year-old "kid/punk," but I always loved great hardcore Rock and Roll!!!! Unfortunately for me, the American music industry at that time was in a DISMAL state of being. The majority of the population was listening to DISCO, the Village People, Donna Summer, the Bee Gees. The BIG movie at the time was *Saturday Night Fever*, and as the Bee Gees said, "Everyone Should Be DANCING," except I didn't want to dance!!!! I wanted to ROCK!!!!!!

One day I was in my office, doing some paperwork and listening to the radio, when all of a sudden I heard this strange noise!!!! It was a loud, blaring, air raid warning siren!!!!! I said to myself, "OH SHIT!!!! ARE WE BEING ATTACKED???!!!" But then I heard a *BUMP BUMP BUMP BUMP* and realized that YES!!!!! My senses, my body, and my soul were being attacked by four local homeboys/musicians from Pasadena, California. They called themselves "VAN HALEN" WOW!!!!!!! The song was "Runnin' with the Devil." Then the guitar chords hit me!!!! The guitar was RAW, CRUDE, NASTY, but TASTY!!!! I'd never heard ANY guitar sound like that before!!! Then the singer's vocals hit me!!!! ALSO RAW, CRUDE, NASTY, but TASTY!!!! Never heard ANY singer sound quite like that before. The rhythm section was tight as could be, and the background vocal harmonies were right on the button.

The next song started, and I heard guitar playing like NO ONE ON THIS EARTH ever played before!!! "ERUPTION"!!!!! OH MAN!!!! WAS THIS GREAT!!!!! It was so incredible it was actually SICK!!!!

For the finale, the radio station played "You Really Got Me," an old Kinks song, but Van Halen's version KICKED ASS on the original Kinks version!! At least I thought so. I WAS SOLD!!!! MY MOUTH WAS OPEN!!! Not only did I love what I heard, but I thought, "These guys are going to be HUGE and going straight to the TOP!!!" And I wanted to go there with them!! Right there, I said to myself, "I gotta work with these guys!!!"

I started shooting Rock photos back in 1969, and one of my "strategies" as a Rock photographer was to always try to have foresight to be able to realize what artists were going to make it and try to hook up with them when they were small and unknown, because once a band starts making it big, EVERY photographer wants to work with them. I did this with Ted Nugent AND Aerosmith and now I had my sights on Van Halen. I HAD TO WORK WITH THEM!!!!

And, a few weeks later, I was going to have my chance!!! At least I thought so. It was now summer 1978, and a couple of photographers I was working with at the time and I were hired to shoot a huge outdoor concert in Texas called "Texas Jam." Scheduled to play were Aerosmith, Ted Nugent, Heart, Journey, etc., etc., and the ALMIGHTY VAN HALEN. Because we were hired by the promoter, we had total access to everyplace, everything, and everyone. At least I thought so...

It was a blistering 115 degrees outside!! I was onstage about ten minutes before Van Halen was to go on, and I was really excited, when all of a sudden the most intimidating human being I have ever seen in my life approached me. He was only about 5-foot-3, but was wearing a black leather coat, skin-tight black pants, "kick your ass" black boots, black leather gloves, Peter Fonda *Easy Rider* aviator sunglasses, a pair of handcuffs on his belt, and—I believe he had some Mace and a billy club. As he was approaching me, I thought "Oh shit. What the FUCK did I do now????" He came up two inches from my face and said, "Who the FUCK are you, what are you doing, and why are you here???" I said I was shooting for the promoter and had total access and was approved to be onstage to shoot the whole set for all the bands. In a very professional BUT very intimidating way, he said "Yeah, all the bands and their whole set EXCEPT FOR VAN HALEN," and said, "Get the FUCK out of here right now!" I SPLIT A.S.A.P. with my tail between my legs!! I was really devastated at not being able to photograph the band that I thought was going to be the next huge success. BUT by not being able to shoot them, I had the opportunity to go into the audience to check out the band and see what they had and if they could "deliver the goods." And they did not disappoint me one bit!!! From the second they hit the stage, they had the crowd, AND ME, in the palms of their hands. IT WAS BRUTAL!!! THEY DESTROYED ALL!!!! NOW, I wanted to—needed to—work with them more than ever!!!

A week after the Texas show, I decided to call their publicist, Bob Gibson (who I had known for years), and said "I want to work with your band, Van Halen." He said, "Okay, they're playing some local Los Angeles shows. I'll get you a photo pass, and you can shoot them live." And so a week later I was driving down to San Diego to shoot a VH headline show, and the next night out to Long Beach to shoot another VH headline show. Once again, the band delivered the goods, and I guess no other photographers had the foresight to shoot them, 'cause I was the only one photographing them at those shows. A few weeks later they were playing a Day on the Green show at the Oakland Coliseum and I decided to fly up to shoot them live, PLUS I was able to set up a QUICK five-minute session before they went onstage. I posed them against a yellow, orange, and green background that was backstage, and I did my usual Zloz yelling-and-screaming routine to try to get some "rock and roll" attitude out of them, and I think they were a little taken—overwhelmed—by the way I was working with them. I really don't think they ever had a photographer work with them like that before!!!

I realized then that I really liked the boys. Honest, down-home, no-bullshit guys. And as we kept working together I found myself getting closer to them as friends more than anything else. I was living in an apartment in Los Angeles at the time and I would be home and, without warning, there would be a random knock at my door and when I said "Who's there?" the reply would maybe be "It's Dave," or "It's Al," or "It's Ed." They would just pop by unexpectedly to hang with me if they were in my neighborhood, and that was COOL!!!!!

The REAL deal that hooked me up with the boys was when they were shooting the photos for their second album, *Van Halen II*. I thought the photographs on *Van Halen* were smoking red hot!!! Very unique and trend-setting at the time, and I guess the boys did too, so they hired the same photographer to shoot the session for *Van Halen II*. They were doing the session at a big soundstage in Hollywood, and the guys asked me if I would like to come down and hang with them, and I said "SURE!!!!" So, I go down to Zoetrope Studios in Hollywood off McCadden and Santa Monica, and there's the photographer on a BIG HUGE soundstage with TONS of assistants and TONS of equipment!!!

BOY was I impressed!!!! First was Al doing his "drum kit on fire" shot, and while the photographer was shooting I was hanging with the band outside. They were all in makeup, so I was doing some impromptu shots in the parking lot. That's where the "Dave jumping off Ed's Peugeot" shot came from, and yes, that's what Ed was driving when I met him!!! Then it was Dave's turn for the album session, and the photographer had him do his famous "TEN MILE HIGH JUMPS" from off the drum riser, over and over. Unfortunately, after the tenth or twelfth jump Dave came down hard and broke his ankle, and even though they weren't done with all the photos, they had to call off the session.

A few days later, the band looked at the shots that were taken and weren't quite happy with them. A few days after that, I got a phone call from the art director at Warner Bros. Records, who said that the band really liked me and felt quite "comfortable" with me and asked me if I would like to finish the project, and I said "SURE!!!!!" So I brought the boys into my studio at the time and I did my "thing" and pulled off the rest of the photos on *Van Halen II*. All the photos except the Alex shots and the Dave jumping on the back cover are mine, and I must say, the nurses we had taking care of Dave were very "tasty." YUM YUM!!!

From 1978 to 1984, Van Halen conquered the world!!!! As far as I'm concerned, they DEVASTATED every other American Rock band that preceded them, and to this day no other American Rock band has come close to the standards that they have set musically or with their offstage antics. They are the ultimate "musicians/entertainers" and have set a standard in the music industry that will be IMPOSSIBLE to touch.

So, that was the beginning of my BEAUTIFUL, EXTRATERRESTRIAL, UNBELIEVABLE, UNIMAGINABLE, ONCE IN A LIFETIME, OH MY GOD EXPERIENCE that no human being could ever hope to experience in their lifetime on this planet Earth!!!! Was it REAL or was it a DREAM???????? I don't know and I don't care!!!!!! BUT, hopefully this book will give you a little peek at the beauty, the magic, and the mystery that I got to experience as their friend and as a photographer!!!!

LONG LIVE VAN HALEN!!

LOVE YOU ALL!!!!

— Neil Zlozower

...AND SOMEONE SAID FAIR WARNING LORD WILL STRIKE THAT POOR BOY DOWN, TURNED FROM HUNTED INTO HUNTER WENT TO HUNT SOMEBODY DOWN...

FUCK OFF ZLOZ

In the Beginning...

It was approximately 1977 when I first met Van Halen at the Whisky a Go Go.

This was before they had a record deal or any actual fans other than the keg-drinking party crowd in Pasadena, California, where they resided. I was a 21-year-old who had recently driven across the country from New York City to Hollywood.

Mario Maglieri, a Mafioso type from Chicago who was the owner of the Sunset Strip's legendary Rainbow Bar and Grill as well as the world-famous Whisky a Go Go, took a liking to me during my job interview, probably because we both sported pompadours. After some verbal jousting, he gave me a job at the Whisky as the assistant manager and lighting director.

Basically, I knew nothing about the responsibilities of either position, but I did know this: there were a lot of very attractive waitresses and only three male employees at the club, so the chances of having contact with female genitalia seemed pretty good.

On a quiet Tuesday night, an unsigned, unknown band from Pasadena was scheduled to perform.

The singer was a blond-haired egomaniacal type who seemed like he was either on speed or practicing to be an aerobics instructor. With long surfer hair, skintight leather pants, open shirt, profuse sweating, and non-stop crotch thrusting, he didn't seem human so much as a one-man porno-circus.

The guitarist was doing things that were completely new to the sound of rock 'n' roll. He was a musical and melodic assault on the senses and a force to behold. The drummer seemed barbaric and prepared to physically attack anyone and anything at any time, but made do by aggressively beating his drums. The bass player seemed like a nice guy who would have been just as happy at home, sitting on a Toro lawn mower with a Budweiser in his hand.

Unfortunately, for all the energy and activity they were putting out on the stage that night, they didn't have more than three paying customers. With the exception of the waitresses, a few stragglers and myself, the room was empty.

I was sitting in the upstairs sound booth sharing some Jack Daniels with the soundman when, at the conclusion of their performance, David Lee Roth arched his back until his long mane of sweat-drenched hair touched the stage and screamed into the microphone, "Make sure you all come back tomorrow night!" I grabbed the microphone in the sound booth, switched on the talkback and responded, "We have to, asshole. We all work here."

I was fired immediately for insulting the group, but on my way out of the club, David asked me to join him for a drink. As we drank late into the night, we got to know each other, spoke about my background and my experience directing short films and art, and his aspirations of world domination. Before we parted ways, he invited me to join the band for rehearsals in the basement of his father's sprawling mansion in Pasadena.

As time passed in the basement rehearsal space, the five of us spent time working on the show, presentation and lighting effects, later incorporating those elements into a showcase for Warner Bros. Records. The band eventually got signed and asked me if I would be interested in traveling with them as a creative consultant and lighting director for their first tour.

One minute I was simply trying to figure out a way to have some intimacy with a waitress in an empty nightclub and the next minute I was traveling down the highway, led by an escort of police motorcycles, with a caravan of five touring busses carrying four musicians, eight security guards, nineteen roadies, an overwhelming number of strippers, "little people" tripping on mescaline, followed by eight semi tractor trailers carrying tons of stage, lighting, and sound equipment, on the way to present the world's biggest rock 'n' roll music party to millions of people.

Live, they were untouchable. We would descend upon a different town every night and they would besiege the stage, grab the audience by the throat and perform their music with relentless passion and power.

The mighty Van Halen was tantamount to a musical and visual tsunami, a Level Five hurricane that left nothing and no one untouched. The music, the performance and the show would annihilate everyone in the arena.

But the real party and insanity started *after* the show. Their dressing rooms were stocked with anything and everything you could imagine, including hundreds of beautiful women, each and every one of them ready, willing and desirous of the depravity du jour.

I spent the next seven years, through 1985, touring the world with Van Halen, designing and directing their lighting and stage shows; directing their videos; designing artwork, merchandise, and album covers; exchanging creative ideas with David; and being a part of one of the most powerful bands in rock 'n' roll history.

It was the beginning of what evolved into a thirty-year career in the music business for me. I am proud of what we created together during those years and have fond memories of experiences that will never be forgotten.

— Pete Angelus

The world's a stage,
and I want the
brightest spot.

– David Lee Roth

1978

Back in 1978, when I first got started working for the band, Dave lived in this old, gigantic mansion in South Pasadena that was probably the biggest house I had ever seen in my life. We did many of the early photo sessions there because you could never run out of ideas with all the different locations and scenery it had to offer.

— Neil Zlozower

I remember Van Halen. Even before I did my radio show at KROQ, they were the house band at Gazzari's. They played every night. I was there with a friend, Hernando Courtright, and we just knew they were gonna be the next big thing. We could tell just by the vibe of the club, always packed and filled with hot females. Girls are constantly setting the trend. Of course, David, with his sense of humor, always carried the band, especially before songs, with his stories.

Then I started my show on KROQ, and had the Ramones on as my first guests. There weren't many local L.A. bands at the time, and I was playing mostly punk and new wave bands like the Runaways, The Quick, and The Pop. Van Halen didn't have a record out at that time, but I knew how popular they were so I got them booked at the Starwood and told Gene and Paul from KISS to come down. KISS were the Heavy Metal Gods of Rock 'n' Roll. Gene loved the band and ended up flying them to New York City to cut some demos, including "Runnin' with the Devil." As soon as they came back to L.A., Dave came on my show as a guest and I played "Runnin' with the Devil" for the first time. I still play that version till this day, along with the David Lee Roth interview on my anniversary show in August, and the phones still keep ringing off the hook!!!!

— Rodney Bingenheimer

My band, Spike, was scheduled to play on a bill that included Orange and The Boyz (featuring George Lynch) at the Starwood in Hollywood. It was rumored that The Boyz had arranged to showcase for Gene Simmons and Paul Stanley from KISS.

At soundcheck, in come the Van Halen Marshall stacks. Eddie had three full stacks with the cover material removed, exposing the wood of the cabinets. They were very distinguishable.

To my surprise, Gene and Paul from KISS showed up — without makeup — and sat down at a table at the Hot 100 Club off-limits celebrity section upstairs. The Boyz did a KISS medley at the end of their set complete with a fog machine under the drum riser. Gene and Paul were not impressed. They decided instead to take Van Halen to New York to record and began what led up to them getting a record deal on Warner Bros.

I heard that the main reason they chose Van Halen over The Boyz was because they thought Roth was a stronger frontman than the singer Lynch had in his band. It was three nights of bombastic, knock 'em dead, winner-take-all hard rock, and Van Halen won!

— Juan Croucier

From the first time I saw Van Halen playing to a small crowd at the Starwood in L.A., and then brought Gene there on my second night, I knew there wasn't a stage they couldn't and wouldn't dominate. They were world-class then and have remained it throughout their career. They've been shamelessly copied, but never close to duplicated.

— Paul Stanley

Once upon a time, when it meant something to be a rock star and groupies prided themselves on whom they had spent the night with, I was invited to the Starwood Club in L.A. to see a band called The Boyz. I took Bebe Buell, she of *Playboy*/Liv Tyler/etc. fame, and sat next to Rodney Bingenheimer, king of the L.A. nightlife, and waited for the opening band to come on.

Life is what happens to you when you least expect it. I saw Van Halen. I was stunned. They killed.

Within two songs I was waiting for them backstage and immediately offered to sign them and take them into the studio. It seems there was a — I kid you not — yogurt manufacturer who was waiting to finance the band. I begged them not to do that. And, in a short time, I flew them to New York, signed them to my Man of 1,000 Faces production company and took them into Electric Ladyland Studios to do a thirteen-song demo. I also bought Dave some platform shoes and leather pants.

I took the demo and showed it to the rest of the KISSers and Bill Aucoin, our then-manager. No one got it. I was shocked. I gave the demo back to the band, told them I had a tour to go on and afterward I would try to get them a record deal, but until then, I tore up our contract and set them free. It didn't take them long to get on Warner Bros.

Did I discover Van Halen? Nah . . . I was there. I saw. I knew. I am a fan.

— Gene Simmons

In the fall of 1976, it was opening night at the Whisky a Go Go, which had been closed to live rock bands for several years due to the current disco trend. Prior to that fortuitous opening, Elmer Valentine, one of the partners of the club and one of my closest friends, called me and asked if I would help him launch the opening of the Whisky by booking bands into the club.

The new wave/punk music scene was starting to gain ground out of London and Los Angeles. I called Kim Fowley, a man who was very much in touch with the local music scene, and asked him if he would produce some shows for us. Kim was very smart and started bringing in some of L.A.'s top bands. The Whisky was off and running again.

A few months later, during the early part of 1977, Kim called me and told me about a band out of Pasadena called Van Halen. I asked him for a contact number so that I could book the band into the Whisky. Kim told me to call Dave Roth, the singer/spokesman of the band. When I got Dave on the phone and introduced myself to him, he was excited that I wanted his band to play the club and invited me to see them play that Friday night at the Pasadena Civic Center.

Arriving at the auditorium I was thinking to myself, "What in the world was a local band doing playing in a three-thousand-seat venue?" As I got to the entrance, there were so many kids waiting to get in that I could not understand what was going on. The place was so packed that the ushers closed the front doors and wouldn't let me in. I went around back to the stage entrance and identified myself to security, and they let me in. I went out front into the audience, where the place was so packed I couldn't move.

All of a sudden the lights went out, the audience started screaming as the band was introduced, and the place went nuts! I could not believe my eyes and ears. There have been many times in my music career that I saw something for the first time that blew my mind, but I was not prepared for what was unfolding right in front of me. The hair on the back of my neck stood out and for the next forty-five minutes I saw the guitar-shredding playing of Edward Van Halen backed by the best rhythm section I've ever heard. Dave Roth was the most amazing frontman/singer I had ever seen. His showmanship coupled with the baddest-ass trio of musicians was a formula that had success written all over it. After the show I went backstage and introduced myself to Dave and the brothers. As I gave Dave a contract for the band to play the Whisky I said, "You guys should have a record deal." My statement probably seemed like bullshit to them, but I told them that I would help them get one and they said, "Sure, go ahead."

Unknown to me, just prior to that evening, Gene Simmons had recorded a demo with the band using his own money and was trying to shop the demo for a record deal. For some reason, no one in the record business was interested. I had a past relationship with some executives at Warner Bros., and after working with the band for a couple of months I called my friend Ted Templeman, one of the greatest record producers in the business, and a genius with vocal harmonies. Ted was working with the Doobie Brothers and I thought he would be the perfect producer for Van Halen.

I had set up a show at the Starwood nightclub in Hollywood on a Monday evening and invited Ted to come and see the band. Ted showed up with Mo Ostin, the chairman of Warner Bros. It was pouring rain that night, and there couldn't have been more than ten people in the audience. I told the band I was bringing some record executives to see them and they kicked royal ass again! When the show was over, Ted and Mo asked me to take them back to the dressing room, which I did, introducing them to the band. Ted and Mo were so blown away they offered the band a record deal right on the spot. For the next eighteen months I worked with Van Halen as their personal manager, and the first album we recorded for Warner Bros. turned out to be the band's biggest-selling album, with over 15,000,000 copies sold.

– Marshall Berle

August, 1977. I was spending my mornings as a Warner Bros. Senior VP, afternoons recording the Doobie Brothers, and evenings playing in Randy Newman's band at the Universal Amphitheater. Then I'd rush over to mix Nicolette Larson's record. Marshall Berle told me about his band and I took a break from mixing, grabbed Mo Ostin, and headed to the Starwood. Five steps in the door and I was hit with the lightning bolt. The guitar player. I knew this was it. The third of the greats. Parker, Tatum, and this guy. Cut the deal that night.

After demoing a lot of songs, we cut the record in two weeks. Dave sang live in a booth, Ed played every solo live in the studio, and we got every one by the third, or usually first, take. I sang backgrounds a lot with Ed and Mike. That was pretty much the drill for the next few recordings. The guys were always sweet, and we had a hell of a time.

— Ted Templeman

I still remember the night in 1978 when my friend rushed over to my house and insisted I listen to this album by this new, unheard-of band. He promised it was going to blow my mind. Well, he wasn't wrong. The power emanating from the speakers was undeniable and immense. I'd never heard anything like it, and as a guitarist I was completely floored and inspired by Eddie's technique and ideas.

— Vivian Campbell

The first time I saw Van Halen it changed the way I looked at music and performing forever. It was 1978 and I had just formed my own group, Dokken. We were opening up for them for two nights at the Starwood in Hollywood. I was standing in my dressing room when they went on. Their first record wasn't out yet, but they hit the stage like they had already made it. I could hear this blistering solo playing that sounded like a guy playing a violin through a Marshall, so I ran out of my dressing room to see what was up and spent the rest of the night watching the show with my mouth hanging open.

Eddie was playing with both hands on the neck. This was the first time I had seen anybody do this. I think he was playing this homemade guitar and an Explorer that night. After that I knew I should give up my guitar playing and just concentrate on my singing because there was no way I could ever attempt to do what he was playing. It was the biggest, punchiest guitar sound I had ever heard. Then, to top it off, there was David Lee Roth, doing his antics and performing like he owned the world. He was so in control of the audience you woulda thought they were on their third world tour. It was scary for me and the rest of the musicians there that night. Van Halen showed everyone they were going to change the face of rock music and take themselves all the way to the top. It was pure attitude.

— Don Dokken

Summer 1978. Hearing them for the first time was one of those events I remember well. I was listening to the radio, waiting to turn left at the intersection of Camino de la Costa and Palomar Ave. on our way to check out the waves at the beach. As if from outer space, like an asteroid was approaching us, the intro to "Runnin' with the Devil" faded up, and launched a phenomenon – Van Halen. The album was sold out, but my surfing friend's older brother had a copy. So, pre-empting *The Twilight Zone*, I listened to the whole album through headphones on his dad's stereo, which looked like the panel from a WW II bomber. It sounded awesome. Ratt guitarist Robbin Crosby had seen them at the Whisky and Starwood clubs and had met Eddie, whose guitar sound at that time was produced in part by running Marshall amplifiers as close to the breaking point as possible. He was going through them like dragster engines and needed spares for a San Diego Arena show. Seeing Robbin's Marshalls up on the stage sparked the thought that we were somehow going to be woven into this rock 'n' roll tapestry someday.

— Warren DeMartini

Van Halen first opened for me in 1978 and it was rock 'n' roll luv at first sight/sound. Coming from the belly of the R&B and R&R beast, I was instantly smitten with the raw energy, attitude, spirit and astonishing virtuosity of all four members. As a direct descendant of the mighty Motown Funk Brothers, I deeply appreciated how Michael and Alex created a Gods of Thunder rhythm section shoulder to shoulder with Eddie's astonishing guitar work and David's James Brown meets Mick Jagger meets Black Oak Arkansas' Jim Dandy meets Wayne Cochran frontman supremacy. All this with a piss-and-vinegar spirit off the damn Richter scale. The Motor City Mad Man was genuinely moved. Even though my amazing band was untouchable, we nonetheless paid close attention to these young smartass dynamos and consciously kicked our performance up a notch or ten right then and there. Van Halen is indeed one of the greatest American rock bands of all time. Godspeed, boys.

— Ted Nugent

I saw Van Halen on their first album tour when they opened for Ted Nugent. Van Halen eclipsed Nugent, something I never thought I would see. David Lee Roth acted like the entire audience was there to see them, which by their next tour would be the case. I remember how collectively stunned the several-thousand-strong audience was after Eddie played "Eruption." Arena rock was never the same after Van Halen came to town. They changed the entire landscape. Neil was there.

— Henry Rollins

I remember hearing about Van Halen from a friend in L.A. in 1977. Then I saw them at the Starwood around that time and got a chance to meet David Lee Roth. I asked him if he'd like to smoke a joint, and yes he did. After that, I was always going up to L.A. to see them. They were insane, to say the least. I was more of a guitar player/singer at the time. I collected rare, hard-to-find amps. I wanted to know what Eddie was using, where, how, and what. I finally got to meet him before a Whisky gig and we got to talking about gear. I had a Vox 30 amp and he used one too but needed another to complete his double-swivel Vox setup. So he bought mine. We became good friends trading, buying, lending gear all the time. I learned a lot from Van Halen, and to this day still think they are one of the best bands to ever hit the world music scene.

— Stephen Pearcy

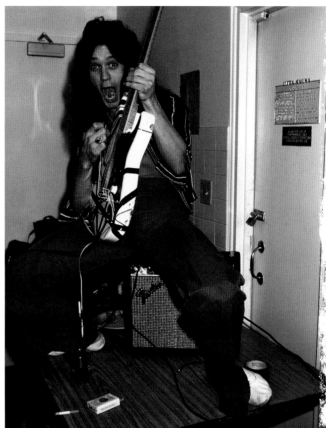

Eddie was the original guitar ninja. At a time when I was just getting my feet wet, he was destroying everything we thought we knew about playing. The first three records are obviously my favorite because I come from a very heavy background. They had those leads and riffs – those heavy fucking riffs – that made us mere mortals wanna give the fuck up. They wrote great heavy rock tunes and were all too happy to force-feed them down our throats.

I saw them six times on the first three records. I remember just sitting in the loge with my binoculars taking in as much as I could from Eddie Van Halen, the motherfucking guitar ninja, and trying to learn about musicianship and showmanship. In their prime, they were untouchable as a live act and, to this day, those shows mean a lot to how I matured as a musician . . . if you want to call it that!

– Kerry King

Eddie's finger tapping and vibrato work were innovative. It's something he developed that made him different than all other guitar players. Extremely different. He mastered it very well. Eddie proves a fellow can create his own thing, something that's recognizable. It's very intriguing, and it's a great road to go down. It's good to see someone out there that plays HIS way. That is what makes the man stand out from the boy.

Eddie Van Halen came up with his own thing. OK. As far as I know, he may have copied it from some hillbilly, I don't know. But it seems like he had his own thing going. And that alone, by itself, makes it very interesting. And the fact that he does it very well means he's expressing a lot of things he had inside him that others don't have. They just don't play that way.

— Les Paul

I heard "Runnin' with the Devil" and nearly shat myself!

— Joe Elliott

The first time I saw them was when they changed their name from Mammoth to Van Halen and added David Lee Roth. They had a tremendous impact on me. Edward is one of the greatest guitarists on the planet. Van Halen changed the sound and direction of rock 'n' roll!

— Mick Mars

After playing with Derringer in the late '70s — where I remember Van Halen coming to see us at the Whisky and Starwood — I moved to L.A. and had a band called Axis. People kept telling me about Van Halen before their first record was released. They said, "This band is your competition." I finally went to see them at the Whisky one night and I was totally blown away with how good they were, especially Eddie. Those guys just fuckin' tore it up! I will never forget it.

— Vinny Appice

I vividly recall the first time I heard Eddie Van Halen perform. Judas Priest had the pleasure to share the same stage with Van Halen in the late '70s in Santa Monica, California, a short time after the release of their first record. I had the great opportunity to watch Eddie's incredible live performance. Right away, I felt this guitar player was going to change the face of rock 'n' roll. His technique and style were a revolution that has influenced and inspired guitarists around the world. Van Halen's legacy remains solid and valuable, and the music will always be around to kick our ass!

— Rob Halford

The mighty Van Halen. I first saw them open for Black Sabbath at the Hammersmith Odeon, 1978. They had a PR gal with them who was a complete bitch. She treated us photographers with contempt. She wanted photographers to sign a contract (this was unheard of at the time). Fuck her. None of us shot the show, but I went out to watch them. They played for forty-five minutes and acted like the Mongol hordes conquering Europe. The funniest part was David Lee Roth telling the crowd of smelly Sabbath fans that Hammersmith is "THE ROCK 'N' ROLL CAPITAL OF THE FUCKING WORLD!" I shot them when they came back headlining the Rainbow Theatre. It was one of the best shows I've ever seen and, yes, Dave did tell us "THE RAINBOW IS THE ROCK 'N' ROLL CAPITAL OF THE FUCKING WORLD!" And for the seventy-five minutes they played, he was right.

— Ross Halfin

I first saw Van Halen at the Rainbow (no, not the L.A. one, the old London one, a big theater) back in 1970-something and I thought they could have been louder. Well, I always think it can be louder! Apart from that, they were excellent: an ultimately impressive frontman (athletic in spandex extremis), the mighty Ed burning the strings off his guitar, and the rock of a rhythm section. Killer show and excellent songs, too. People said, "Aaargh, they got big hair!" I said, "If they sound that good, I don't care if they got five buttocks! Each!" I believe that if Dave gets back on stage with Van Halen, they will sound just as good! Maybe even better!

— Lemmy

It was 1978 and the Van Halen boys were to play at an outdoor gig up in Oakland, California, at Bill Graham's Day on the Green Festival. They were opening for some bigger bands and were to play early in the day. This was to be my first offstage session with the band and I was pretty STOKED, so I set my alarm clock for Sunday morning (at least I thought so), but next thing you know I'm waking up . . . one hour later than I planned! SHIT, the alarm didn't go off! So I grab my equipment (no shower) and jammed in my 'Stang down La Brea to the airport at about 80 miles an hour. I get there about ten minutes before the flight is supposed to leave and find out that the plane is about one hour delayed! LUCKY ME! I make the flight, get off at Oakland, get to the gig about fifteen minutes before the band goes on, and I say, "OK GUYS, LET'S SHOOT!" We shot about thirty six frames and the band took the stage and DEVASTATED every other band that played on the bill that day.

THEY WERE BRUTAL!

– Neil Zlozower

It is only the most elite of elite musicians whose unconventional approach becomes convention.

– Steve Vai

1979

When I first heard "Runnin' with the Devil" on the radio, I was stunned and found myself dizzy, walking through my high school hallways thinking, "What was THAT?!"

Eddie Van Halen was so innovative and kicked so much ass, and David Lee Roth was for a time indisputably the Greatest Man in America.

If aliens came down and challenged us to a Battle of the Bands to decide the fate of Planet Earth, I would feel very confident putting early Van Halen forward as our champion.

— Tom Morello

Guitarists of the previous generation might have been asked the question, "Where were you the first time you heard Jimi Hendrix?"

For the players of my generation, the question must certainly be, "Where were you the first time you heard Eddie Van Halen?"

For me, that musical moment was as astounding as the what/where/how of hearing that JFK had been shot (FYI, I was traveling to the library on a public bus watching grown men weep over portable AM radios). I was invited to spend the evening at a buddy's house for a party. He had recently lost his parents and inherited a shitload of cash. In his grief and a mental state that I would describe as "numb as much pain as possible," he was treating us all to tons of booze and this stuff called coke. I was certainly a novice to both. With a gathering of about twelve boys and girls, we proceeded to drink lots of Jack Daniels and sniff "that white stuff."

At the time, Led Zep's *Houses Of The Holy*, Boston, Aerosmith's *Rocks,* and my favorite geetar player at the time, Jeff Beck, were on constant rotation. Then my buddy put on this new band, Van Halen. He didn't give me a primer of any sort ... it just came on matter of factly. Right before Ed's "Eruption" solo started, my buddy yelled out to me, "Steve, you should listen to this." Talk about an understatement. I didn't even allow twenty seconds to go by before dashing for the turntable (ahh, the good ol' days) and lifting the needle to start the track over from the beginning again.

Did I hear that correctly? Was that a guitar or a mini-Moog? A human? Now, I knew of plenty of technically great players before this. Uli Roth from the Scorpions was pretty badass. I had even heard Allan Holdsworth by this time, but this was not some jazzer or prog guy, this was a rock 'n' roll guitar player and he sounded like he was grinning ear to ear. As I listened to the rest of *Van Halen I* that night (about ten times) I could hear lil' bits of cool influences like a snare drum sound that only a Bill Bruford fan would desire. Even so, the game had changed and I could tell the instrument I had already played for eleven years would never ever be the same. I don't know which was worse the day after, my hangover from hell or the realization that I had a whole lot of practicing ahead of me.

Cut ahead years later. I had made my own career with this English guy named Billy Idol and we had this *Rebel Yell* thang goin' on. I was invited to play on a new Michael Jackson song called "Dirty Diana." After Ed recorded "Beat It" with Michael, they needed some flash guitar on the follow-up record and I guess I was their man. The session was a one-afternoon deal and Michael said, "I like the high notes."

The next day I get a call from that Eddie Van Halen guy to come by his house to jam and play at that year's NAMM show. After the initial shock of plugging in to one of Ed's amps, I told him I had just done the Michael Jackson session. Ed said "Hey man, did he say he liked the high notes?" Too fucking funny!

Years later I was playing guitar for Vince Neil of Mötley Crüe. We had recorded our album and were now invited out to support Van Halen. As I had always done, I brought out my thirty-year-old vintage Marshalls on the road ... nervously, I might add. When Ed saw them he said, "Man those are priceless, you should try my new amps at our next soundcheck. If ya like 'em, I will have some sent out." Well the next day with Alex on his kit and Michael Anthony on his bass, Ed hands me his guitar and just like that: I'm in Van Halen now! Ha ha! Suffice to say, the amps sounded fantastic. Two days later, three full stacks arrive by truck. I played those amps for the next ten years. Oh yeah, Ed threw in two guitars just for shits and giggles. Does the word generous even come close to describing this gesture?

Once again, thanks Ed.

— Steve Stevens

Hands down, the greatest AMERICAN BAND of all time. Van Halen came out at the right time.

Music needed a kick in the ass and they got it.

I can't tell you the exact words I uttered the first time I heard Van Halen, but it was something like, "WHAT THE FUCK IS THAT?" My ears and brain could not comprehend what was coming out of the speakers. I knew that this would soon take over the world. This was a new level in entertainment and music, and life was never the same after this. They were musical crack to me.

Seeing them live in 1979 was an experience I will never forget. When I actually saw Eddie playing this stuff in front of me it was as if he was Harry Houdini. He was doing things to the guitar that no one had ever done. This man was from another planet.

Alex Van Halen was a big influence on my drumming. His style and approach were so HUGE (as were his kits). He paved the way for drummers. I still get goosebumps when I hear his snare drum.

VAN HALEN FUCKING RULE!

— Charlie Benante

Rocktober 07, 1979, the Los Angeles Forum, *Van Halen II* tour: there was enough energy in the air to light up the entire West Coast for ten years! The BEST live band I have ever witnessed in my life, period, hands down, end of the mutha-fucking story!

— Joey Allen

Alex has the most unique drum tone ever! A signature sound. Van Halen has the ultimate rhythm section.

— Joey Jordison

Alex the Animal. The first time I heard Van Halen was "Runnin' with the Devil" on the radio on WMMS in Cleveland. I remember thinking (along with everyone else), "Who the hell is this, and who is this guitarist?" Well, we all know they went on to open for Black Sabbath and really give them a run for their money.

By the time the second Van Halen record hit, I finally got to see the new kids on the block live. And ALIVE they were! I had never seen a band come on stage with such energy and fire. Not to mention the sheer power that they each presented on their instruments. Eddie had opened the door for the band with his groundbreaking style, but the rest of the band were no sideshow either. Especially Alex.

This guy was all over the kit from the opening to the end of the night and, if I remember correctly, did three different drum solos throughout the show. Even the first song ended with a solo flurry, just to set the tone for the evening.

Alex has always had his own voice on the drums, which is the hardest instrument to achieve that on. From his trademark popping snare sound and high-pitched tom tom tuning to his electronic Simmons phase, on up to the Bonham-esque thunder of "Poundcake," he has retained something unique and special on the instrument that has inspired many a drummer for the past thirty years.

— Eric Singer

I was a ten-year-old kid listening to L.A. radio station KMET when I heard "Eruption." It just blew me away. Then right into the Kinks' "You Really Got Me." Needless to say, I was hooked and pre-ordered the record at my local record store. Twelve years later I ended up working for Mike as his bass tech for five years.

They've always impressed me with how they could take another band's song and make it their own. From Ed's guitar playing, to Dave's vocals and lyrics, to Michael Anthony's background vocals, and Alex's snare drum sound, when you heard two notes of a song you knew it was Van Halen! From 1978 to 1984 no one could hold a candle to Van Halen. I don't think anyone's ever come close!

— Craig DeFalco

As much as I would have loved to play bass in Van Halen, and as close as that may or may not have come to be, I still have to say in all fairness that Michael Anthony was and is an irreplaceable part of Van Halen. He nailed all the high harmonies perfectly and was a solid counterpoint to Ed's playing.

— Billy Sheehan

I will never forget hearing Michael's bass and signature high vocals. He was a gentleman and extremely talented to work with. Without Van Halen, rock music would NOT be the same.

— Bruce Kulick

81

Eddie Van Halen is the master. He's the kind of guy I grew up staring at on MTV thinking, "He has sold his soul to the devil. He has magic in them fingertips!" Van Halen is untouchable because they rock hard, but they have a sense of humor in everything they do. They aren't clowns for your amusement, and enjoy what they do to the extreme, which makes for a spectacular performance.

— Allison Robertson

When I first started hanging with the guys, they would just randomly pop over to my apartment to hang out with me if they were in my neighborhood. Ed had just gotten rid of his old Peugeot and got a brand new CJ Jeep that he really loved. Every time Ed would come over with the Jeep, instead of parking on the street like a NORMAL person, he would always park on the front lawn of my complex. This time, I grabbed a camera and we did a FAST session with him and his prized Jeep.

— Neil Zlozower

Van Halen is the pure embodiment of American Rock: original, outrageous, and you knew when you went to see them live you were gonna have a great time.

As a kid growing up in Detroit, I saw Van Halen many times. I first saw them as the opening act on a three-band bill with Montrose (with Sammy Hagar singing) and a new version of Journey, which had some high-voiced guy named Steve Perry. I thought at the time the other bands were okay, but I was really there to see the wildmen of California. I weaseled my way to the backstage, traded a bag of weed for a pass, and was in rock heaven watching them tear up the place with their sound.

The next time was on the second album tour and they were headlining. They had so much power, and were just having so much goddamn fun. I loved it.

Then the infamous Cobo Hall, Detroit, opening for a tired Black Sabbath. They come on stage and played the first song like it was the encore. After what felt like a five-minute ending, the place went absolutely crazy. David soaks this in and struts to the front of the stage just looking out and smiling, shaking his head, loving it. What seems like another five minutes, he finally steps to the mic and in a slow growl goes, "Fuckin'-A Deeetroit!!!" The place goes completely nuts!

I thought it would be cool to be in a rock band up until then, but after that, I had no choice. I had been to the church of Van Halen and was a card-carrying converted member. It was pure original outrageousness. Pure American Rock.

— Chad Smith

I am astonished by the breadth and scope of Edward's talent. So natural. His playing is raunchy, tasteful, melodic, and unique. He has fun when he plays; there is celebration and joy in his playing. A serious musician who makes magic look effortless, Edward has all the ammunition in his arsenal.

— David Coverdale

Ed is a phenomenal, innovative, and very soulful musician. I say "musician" rather than simply "guitarist" because he is so much more than that. He is one of the last true guitar heroes, yet he's a friendly, down-to-earth guy, and for me, that's probably his most endearing trait.

— Elliot Easton

Eddie likes to present himself as a simple, "aw shucks" kind of guy, but make no mistake, he is nobody's fool. Edward is super-observant, whip-smart, and funny. Not a thing gets by him. He's thought long and hard about the guitar and the music he plays. It may not look that way, because like Fred Astaire, his command and artistry make it look effortless.

His accomplishments are enormous. Positively towering. Without getting geeky, there isn't one aspect of the electric guitar that he hasn't changed, rearranged, or renovated. He's Hendrix and Les Paul combined. He revolutionized the way the guitar is played and revolutionized guitar technology. But the real dirty little secret to Ed's genius is that he's an even better songwriter than he is a player.

— Brad Tolinski

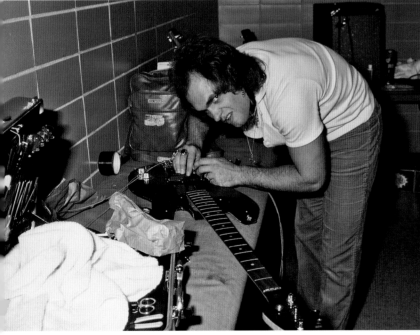

What can I say about my favorite rock 'n' roll band? I have known Ed and Al for a long time and I consider them great soul brothers. We have been through a lot together as friends and musicians and I have had the honor of jamming with them live and doing some studio sessions with Ed. They changed the face and sound of rock 'n' roll in 1978 and it's never been the same since. Ed reinvented the guitar and created a new genre of playing. Few can say that! Al's groove is HUGE and when they all play together, it's magic! Great songs and great playing.

Their music has stood the test of time.

— Steve Lukather

I.S. 25 Junior High lunch room, 1978, and my friend David says, "Wait 'til you hear this!" He pops a cassette tape into his tiny portable radio, pushes play, and the sickest thing I've ever heard erupts from the speakers. Literally. He had cued up "Eruption" and I sat there hypnotized by a sound I had never heard before. All I could muster after the track ended was a weak, "How did he do that?" I'm still wondering.

Van Halen rules.

— Scott Ian

#1: I was a teenager in the '70s and I loved all the heavy metal bands. But they were always FROWNING or angry at something. Van Halen was different. They were having a GOOD TIME and they were PROUD of it. When I saw them live, I got the feeling that those four guys were at that very moment having more fun than ANYONE on the planet Earth. And damn it, I wanted some, too!

#2: I joined my first rock band when I was eleven. I quit because the drummer couldn't play the tom tom lick at the beginning of "D.O.A."

#3: The happiest human beings I have ever seen in my life were Van Halen on stage in 1979. I don't know if it was real, but that's the impression they gave me. And it has stayed with me like a religion.

#4: I have three gods: The Beatles, Van Halen, and . . . OK, I only have two.

#5: I stole a lot of licks from Eddie when I was a kid. Years later I hung out with him at his studio and he played music at such a high volume that I lost a big chunk of my hearing. Those licks were worth it.

— Paul Gilbert

Van Halen was and still is my favorite band of all time. Me and my brother always modeled ourselves after them. They were without a doubt our biggest influence. We had so much in common with them it's unbelievable. The first time I met Eddie Van Halen we just hit it off. We had been talking for a brief time and he looked over at me and said, "I've only been talkin' to you for fifteen minutes and we have so much in common I feel like I've known you a lifetime." I laughed and just said, "You don't know how much we have in common." I always felt like Pantera was the heavy metal version of Van Halen. Without Van Halen, music would have never had charisma!

— Vinnie Paul

To me, Van Halen is the most influential American rock band ever.

– Rick Savage

1980

Ah, what these eyes have seen! I was there, brother, for an insane, four-year 'round-the-world ride. 1980–1984. Director of security. We were kings, gods & no, we were Van Halen. We could do no wrong. The crazier we got, the more you loved us, and the more you loved us, the bigger we got. Nobody could improve on what we'd perfected. The Stones may have been a rock and roll circus but we were a rock and roll zoo. Animals with guitars. Wolves watching over the sheep. Creative chaos. A world invasion with "The Fifty-Five Ton Gun," which is what we called our lighting sound, and stage gear. We were the Jack Daniels Black Label of everything dangerous and desirous.

And yes, it was dangerous. My job description was simply one line: Protect the band. But taking care of David (I was his designated babysitter), Edward, Alex, and Michael, was not always such a simple thing to do. I had to keep them safe when they were playing live. How did I know that the lunatic jumping on stage only wanted to sing along with Dave? I had to keep them out of harm's way when they were back at the hotel, when they were partying, when they were traveling. Berserk fans. Jealous boyfriends. I had to protect them from each other. I had to protect them from themselves.

I look back on it now and it's surreal. My memories seem impossibly crazy. Sold out shows. Drinking. Drugs. Women. Then I remember where I was and who I was and what I did, and I know the recollections don't even come close to the reality. The music was timeless, the attitude pure fucking rock and roll. I could tell you about some of the things that happened. I could describe to you the most outrageously beautiful women in the world lining up outside your hotel room door. I could try and make you understand how it felt to wield this almost unlimited power. Or I could tell you about the time, after a major VH backstage demolishing in Germany, how I had to scrape mustard, mayonnaise, butter, ketchup, relish, and lunchmeats off a hospitality room ceiling because I was fucking starving and they had trashed every other edible morsel in sight. It wasn't always about excess, mind you. Now, I could reveal a lot more about these escapades but then I'd have to beat the shit out of you. And that's not good for me or you—mainly you.

So look at Zloz's photos and they'll describe perfectly what happened. He was there and he saw it all. Maybe, eye-balling our world through one of his Nikon F2s or FEs, he even saw it more clearly than the rest of us. I dealt with a lot of photographers on the road, but no one had the band's trust like Neil did. He was loud and a maniac, but shoot me if he didn't take the finest Van Halen photos ever. Still, I better not see myself in one of his shots, standing atop two stacked wooden chairs, perched upon a wobbly catering table, and using a piece of bread to scrape condiments off a chandelier. There will be hell to pay. . . .

— Eddie Anderson

→1A →2 →2A →3 →3A →6 →6A

→9A →10 →10A →11 →11A →12 →12A

→4 →4A →5 →5A →6 →6A

→10 →10A →11 →11A →12 →12A

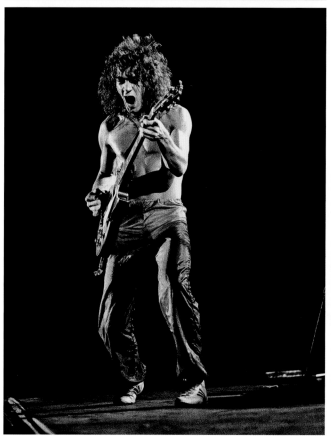
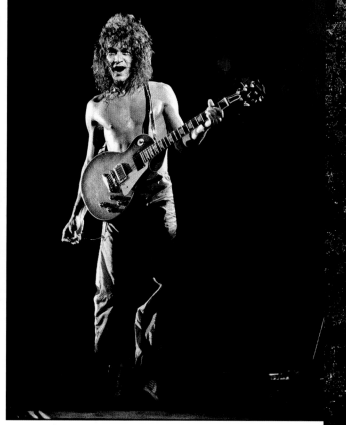

In the winter of 1980, my buddy and I drove through a
blizzard to buy Van Halen tickets for a show at the Spectrum
in Philadelphia. This was before MTV and the Internet, so it
was like a pilgrimage to see your favorite bands. After avoiding
hitting several cars and a few telephone poles, we had our
fourth-row tickets in hand. Several months later we found
ourselves at the concert. My friends and I had been listening
to Van Halen for a few years prior to this, but nothing could
prepare us for what we saw that night.

The show was completely over the top. Huge sound, huge
lights. Dave was doing leaps off of the drum riser. All the
guys in the band are amazing musicians. Being a drummer
myself I always fixated on the drummer, and Alex was beating
the crap out of a drum set that looked more like a spaceship
than a normal drum set.

I attended many more Van Halen shows over the next several
years. Each one was bigger than the previous one. Overall, it
was one of those nights that help you realize what you want
to do with your life. In the fall of 2005, I found myself playing
drums for David Lee Roth. Go figure.

— Jimmy DeGrasso

Women and Children First doesn't receive the credit it
deserves. My uncle played it for me when I was five years
old and I've been a diehard Van Halen fan since. It is a
landmark record in my life and influenced me to pick up the
drum sticks at a very young age. "Take Your Whiskey Home"
is still my favorite Van Halen track. Every time I hear it I run
and get a double!

— Joey Jordison

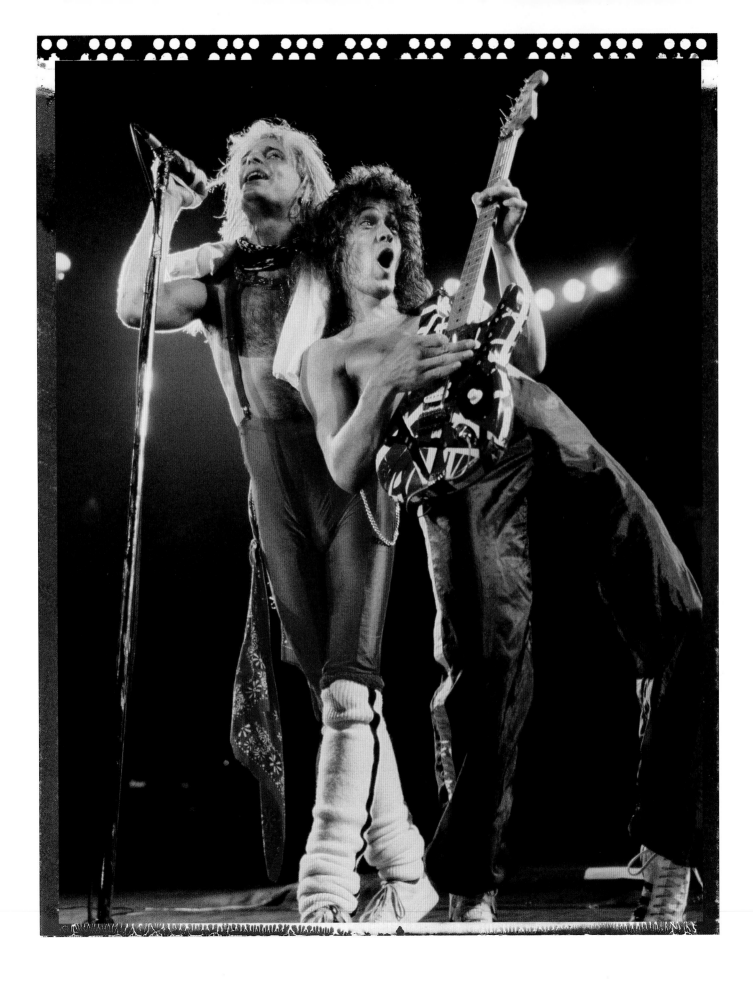

Even as a local band, Van Halen knew their destiny. There were great bands around L.A. and then there was Van Halen, peerless. With ferocious determination they set a new course for the history of rock.

— Grover Jackson

David Lee Roth, in my mind, is one of the greatest rock 'n' roll frontmen of all time, untouchable! Although, the very first time I saw the mighty Van Halen live at Jantzen Beach Center in Portland was another story. Mid-show, the affable Roth reaches down into the surging swarm of hotties in the front to shake and slap some hands and as quickly as you can say jump, he's pulled into the pit and engulfed by a sea of fanatics. The situation gets worse when security, in an effort to rescue the hapless Roth from the pit, pulls him one way and his signature yellow-and-black striped stage pants go the other! The tug-of-war with the now bare-assed Diamond Dave continued for what seemed like eternity before David was finally able to struggle back to the relative safety of the stage with his pants intact!

— Tommy Thayer

In 1980, my band Talas opened up for Van Halen on the *Women and Children First* tour for about forty shows. We went out front to watch the show every night. At their very worst, they were spectacular. At their best, they were utterly untouchable. The show was simply the most exciting, entertaining, and incredible textbook kick-ass rock show ever, the standard by which all others are judged.

— Billy Sheehan

When I did my first photo session with Neil I was in awe of the photos he had of Van Halen. I was lucky enough to see them in concert many times during the Dave era. The first time was on the *Women and Children First* tour. Their showmanship was unreal, but their musicianship was just as good. Alex's drum set was massive, like nothing I'd ever seen before. Eddie was on fire. I couldn't believe someone could be running around and jumping all over the stage and still play like that! Dave was larger than life, the ultimate showman. I wanted to be just like all of them.

They influenced an entire generation of musicians and defined what it means to be a Rock Star. There was a magic with that band that will probably never happen again. You can't really explain it to people who didn't experience it.

— Blas Elias

It was 1980, and I was obsessed with Ted Nugent, KISS, and Bob Seger. A friend's brother kept telling me, "Man, you gotta check out these guys" while holding up *Van Halen I*. But if they weren't wearing makeup or running around in a loincloth I wasn't having it! Well, he sat me down and played me the record and told me I couldn't leave his room until it was over. Holy crap, was I a changed man after that! It was Van Halen time for me. I immediately bought a cheap black Fender guitar and proceeded to put yellow tape all over it. Mind you, I couldn't even tune the thing, but, man, did I look good holding it! Then it was David Lee Roth or bust! I started wearing the bandana on my wrist and the Capezio shoes. All I was lacking was his self-esteem, long blond hair, and the ability to touch my hands to my feet, let alone do the splits off the edge of my bed.

My first Van Halen show was the *Women and Children First* tour at the Forum. I walked away thinking, "Man, David Lee sure is tall!" He seemed twelve feet tall from where I was sitting (loge 12, by the way). He had something that I've never seen in a frontman before, a larger-than-life persona and more ham than Farmer John! All the guys wanted to be him and all the girls wanted to do him. I never missed a show from that point on and it's a pleasure for me to say that I got a chance to become Dave's music publisher in 2001. To be able to look after all of those songs and to deal with him directly is a dream come true for me.

— Mark Friedman

Van Halen is the musical equivalent of the yearly Harley festival in Sturgis. Loud, proud, and always a crowd.

– Rick Nielsen

1981

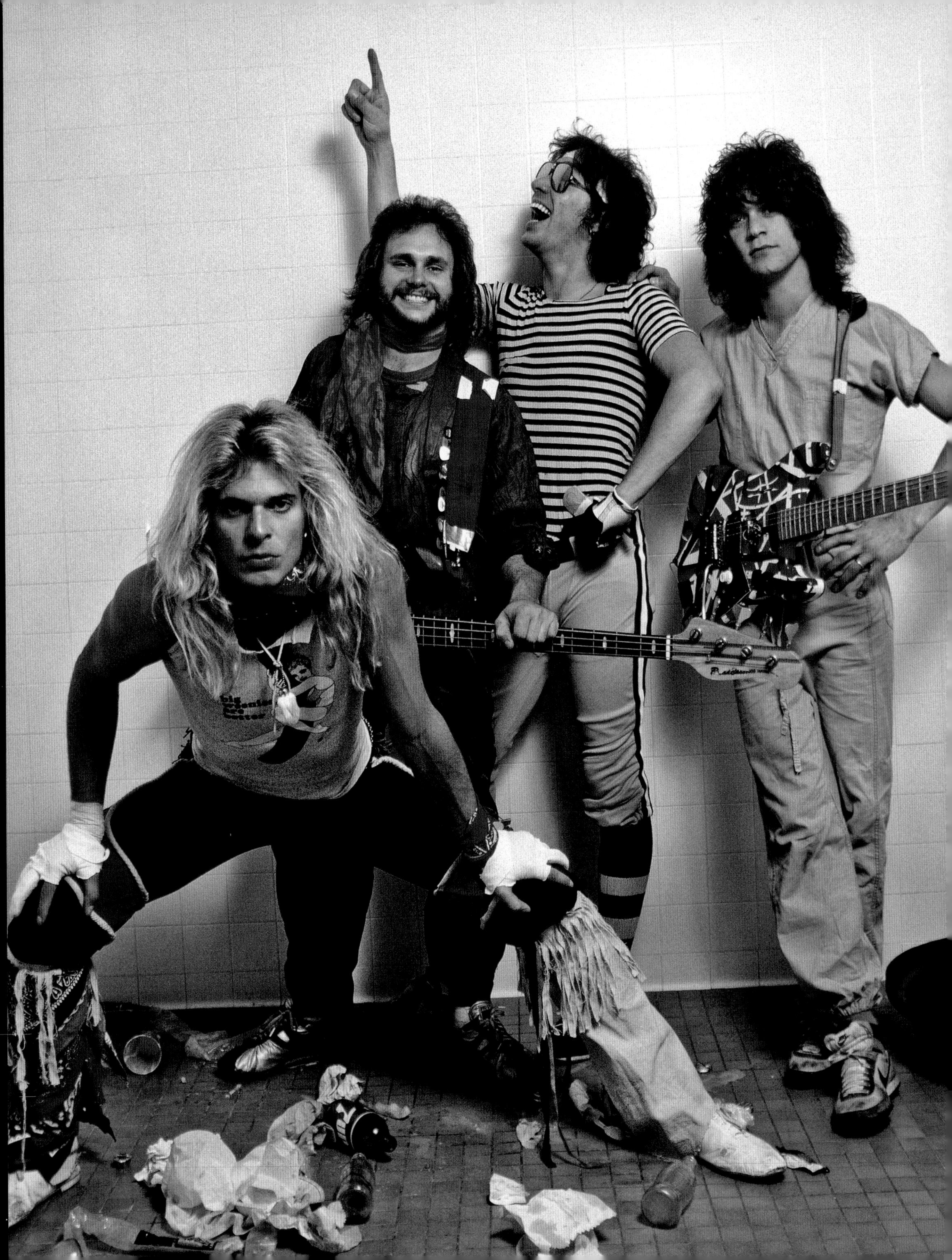

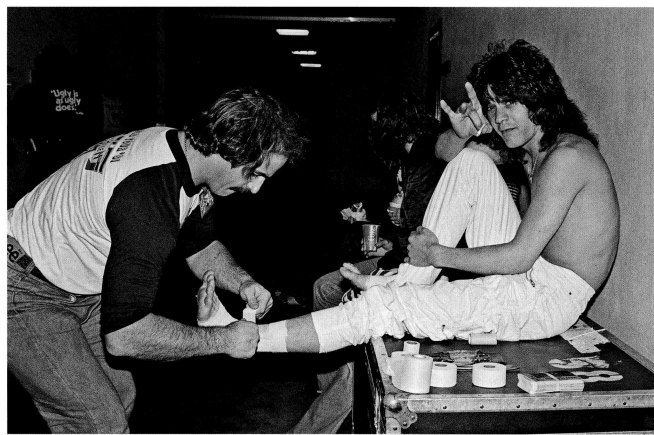

I remember every band in L.A. wearing fuckin' bandanas. That was Dave. I can't remember a world without Van Halen and David Lee Roth. In their day, nobody on earth could even come close. They ruled the planet.

— Jaime St. James

I was already a dedicated Van Halen fan when I met the band in 1981. I was living in Madrid, Spain, and shared the same record company. The band was coming to Spain to promote *Fair Warning* and I asked the record company if I could be part of the team who picked up the band and assisted them while they were here. I ended up going by myself to the airport with three limos to welcome Van Halen, my heroes, to Spain.

So there I was in the airport, not just the welcome committee, but now also the interpreter, and I barely spoke Spanish. Dressed in a Van Halen T-shirt and rocked out to the teeth, I nervously awaited the band's arrival, and who would appear first, none other than God himself, the one and only Diamond David Lee Roth. Now you have to imagine this picture. The airport is packed with Spanish people waiting for their families, thousands of people all with black hair. Then there's Dave and me. Both with long blond hair, both completely out of place. As soon as Dave came out he saw me and we both just stood there for what seemed like a lifetime, staring each other down like two gunfighters in a dusty street, one shaking in his pants, the other calm and cool behind dark sunglasses. It was frightening, but awesome!

Dave came right at me, and I'll never forget the first words out of his mouth, "Who are you? Do you have a joint?" From that moment, the shield was down and I had been welcomed into Dave's world. Then out came Eddie, Alex, and Michael, but what can I say, I had been "Daved" all the way and it was as if nothing else mattered.

That night, the label was taking the band out for traditional Spanish food, but Dave wanted none of it. He asked me to take him to McDonald's, so off we went in a taxi, with Dave telling story after story and me just inhaling everything he said like the master's apprentice. Sitting at McDonald's devouring a tower of cheeseburgers, two Spanish girls came to our table and asked for my autograph. Dave was probably shocked by this, even though he didn't show it. I hadn't told him that I was well-known in Spain and quite popular, especially with the señoritas. I told the girls that Dave was a very famous rockstar from the USA and they should get his autograph, which he in return signed twice as big as mine with a big "Van Halen" added to it. It should be pointed out that VH wasn't well-known in Spain at the time.

After our Golden Arches dinner, we hung out in his room, listening to music, Dave showed me how you attach a chunk of hashish onto the pin in the Van Halen badge he'd given me, then put a glass over it, let it fill up, and suck it all down. He just showed me all the ropes, and that's when Dave told me: "If you want to break America, you gotta play the clubs for ten years." The following year I followed my dream and went to the USA. It only took me five years to break, I guess I had a great master, and he had already paved the way for the rest of us disciples.

Dave also told me, "Life is like a kung-fu movie. It doesn't matter if you win or lose, as long as you look good."

He was my God!

— Mike Tramp

When Dave was at the helm, I don't think there was a bigger Van Halen fan than me. From 1978 to 1980, I lived off mega doses of their records, and scoured over live photos that gave me a peek into the hurricane that was VAN HALEN.

I was thirteen when I first saw them live. It was the 1981 *Fair Warning* tour at the Forum in Los Angeles that lit the fuse for my obsession with rock. The furious power and glory that I witnessed that night was fucking staggering. It was an all-out blistering assault on the senses. With the most high-energy, colorful, witty, kick-ass frontman rock could ask for. Van Halen took me and 18,000 of their closest friends into the rock 'n' roll jungle, never to return the same person again. It was a defining moment for me and rock.

I had been branded with a hot-ass poker, and my path was clear. My ass was not.

— Brad Wilk

The first time I heard Van Halen it was life-altering. Just like Black Sabbath, Led Zeppelin and Jimi Hendrix, the good Lord put them down here to whoop some ass and teach everybody how it's supposed to be done! Dave is the legendary frontman. Eddie is the greatest. You got Hendrix and you got Eddie. Mike is the Rock of Gibraltar and one of the coolest guys ever, and Alex is the foundation of the house. You got John Bonham, Louie Bellson, Buddy Rich, Mitch Mitchell and Ginger Baker. Alex is cut from the same cloth. Long live Van Halen.

— Zakk Wylde

Eddie changed the face of guitar and that should be legend enough, but it was the whole band's devil-may-care musical attitude that really captured my attention. David was brilliant and spawned a new batch of frontmen, but they did it together. What a breath of fresh air. Great band, great guys, great times.

— Ronnie James Dio

The definition of ROCK STAR
is David Lee Roth.
Period, end of story.

– M. Shawn Crahan

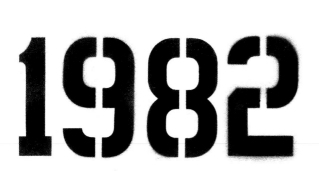

Eddie Van Halen was and is the pinnacle of
Van Halen. His guitar playing transcends the
boundaries of rock 'n' roll guitar, bending all the
rules of traditional techniques. His style quickly
revolutionized the genre and influenced the
next generation of guitar players worldwide.

Not since Jimi Hendrix has there been such an
impact on the way rock 'n' roll guitar is played.
Eddie is one of the greatest guitar players to
ever come along.

There's not much more to say.

— Slash

Van Halen was the first kick-ass rock band, but they weren't afraid to grow musically and experiment. Songs like "Jamie's Cryin'" and "I'll Wait" show they could write more than just rock anthems. Van Halen is the benchmark for the rest of us to achieve.

— James Root

Van Halen changed the rock industry. Not only is Edward far and away the best rock guitarist, David Lee Roth is, hands down, the best frontman in rock history, influencing every aspiring rock band in the world. They are the perfect rock band.

— Kip Winger

Eddie Van Halen and his band of rock 'n' roll animals are in my humble opinion the greatest good time, kick-ass rockers of all time. Cheers to an awesome career!

— Erik Turner

I saw them one summer night at the New Haven Coliseum. Dave stopped the show in the middle of a song and asked for all the lights to be turned off. He sat down in the dark and lit a joint that had been thrown onto the stage from someone in the audience. The crowd went absolutely crazy. It was confirmed: I wanted to be a rock star.

— Miljenko Matijevic

The first time I heard about Van Halen was from my uncle who went to a Black Sabbath concert in Austin, Texas. Van Halen was supporting them on that leg. I don't remember much details, but I do remember him saying, "Van Halen kicked Sabbath's ass!"

When I was in eighth grade, *Diver Down* was the rage, and I finally had a taste of it at a friend's birthday party. It definitely rocked. From the moment "Where Have All the Good Times Gone" began, I enjoyed the guitars and drumming . . . but mostly I was drawn to the vocals. They were wild, alive and real.

It wasn't until *1984* that I saw a Van Halen video, "Hot for Teacher." Being a percussionist, the drum intro blew my mind. Yet it was the antics of David Lee Roth that gave me real appreciation of his talent. In my opinion, David Lee Roth epitomized the frontman of the 1980s. There, I said it.

— Burton C. Bell

The first time I ever met Dave was on the first day of a tour. He was standing there with his back towards me and said, "Hold on, I'll be right with you." Then I realized what he was doing. He was peeing in one of my drum cases!

He was Diamond Dave all the time, but once I was sitting on the bus with him and saw him as David Roth. He was working on one of his paintings. He looked at me and said, "Fred, there are three types of people in this world. Muffins, birds and horses. You're a horse."

— Fred Coury

For my money, Eddie Van Halen was the first
significant new kid on the block. Very dazzling.
He played a vital role in keeping kids interested
in playing guitar, because they could look up to
this cheeky little guy with the big smile.

He flies the flag well, I think.

— Jimmy Page

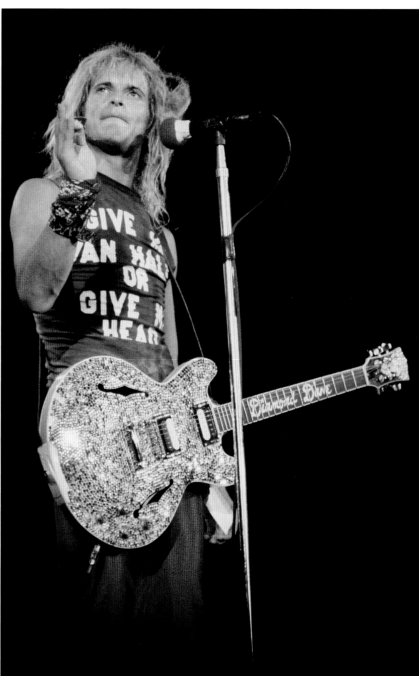

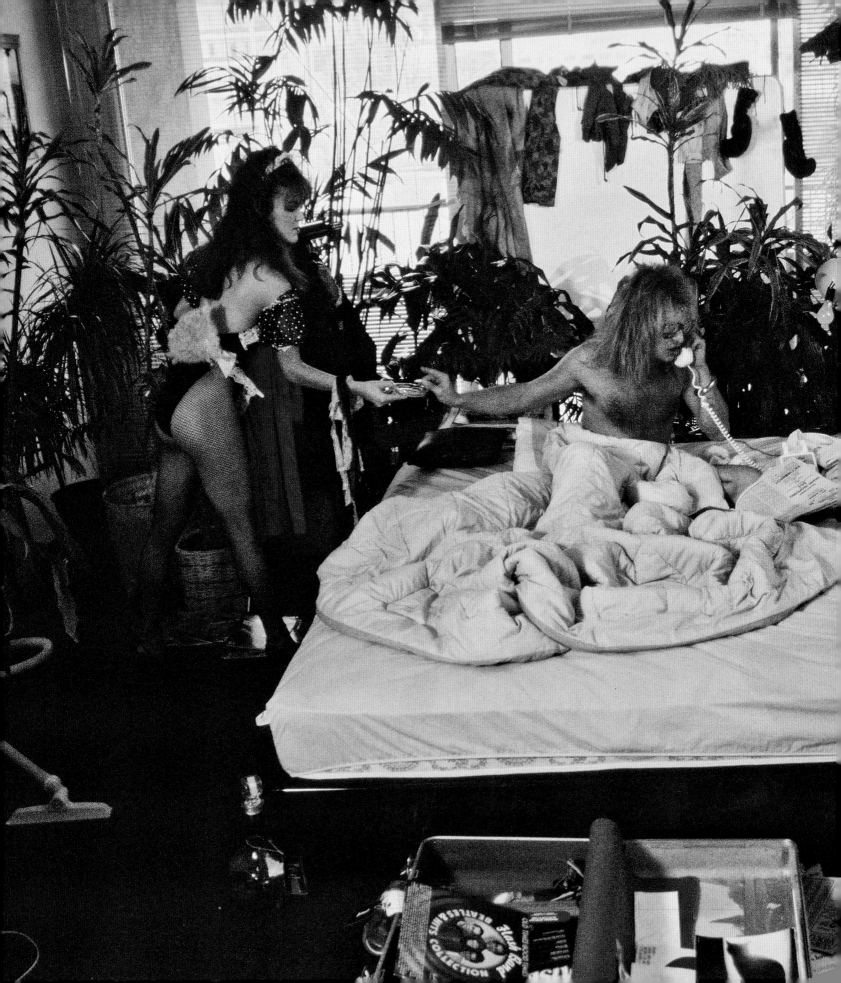

One time I overheard David seriously talking to my mum about dogs and all things domestic. Seemed weird, considering Alex was having a drink-off with one of our guys at the same time.

– Phil Collen

1983

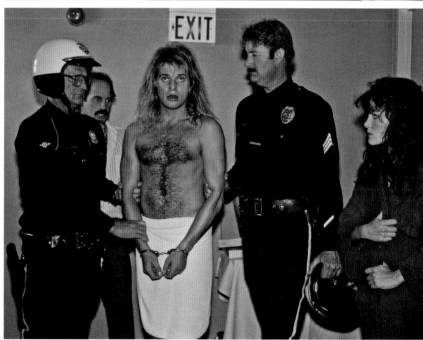

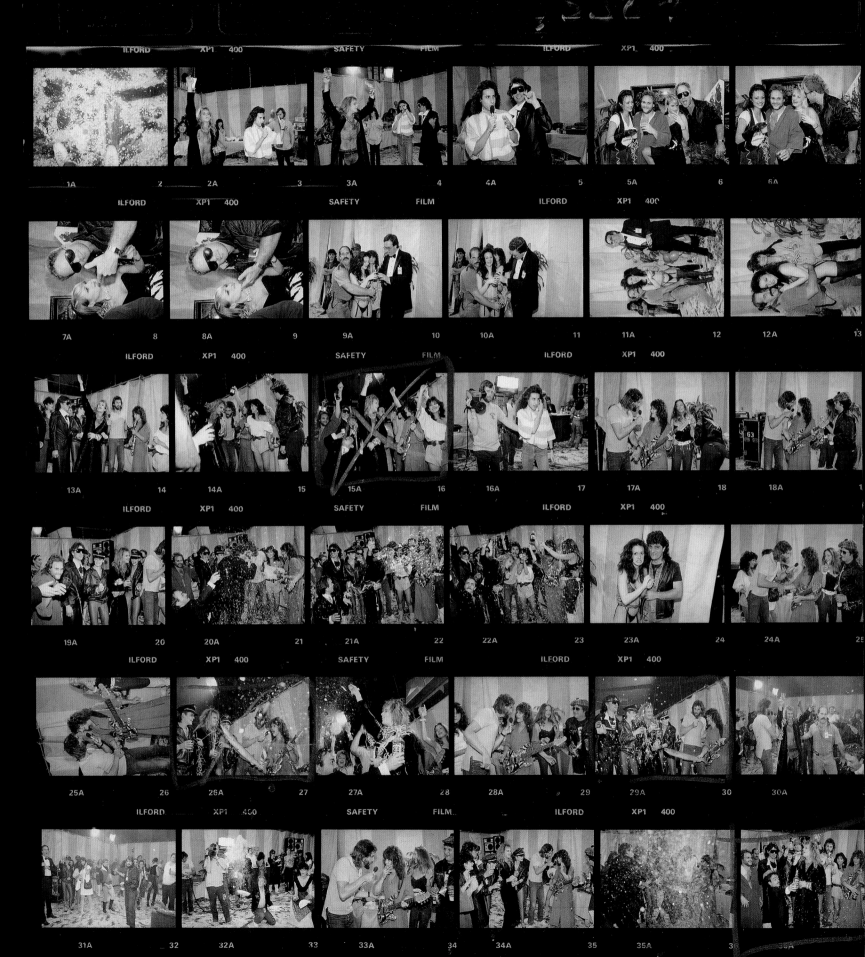

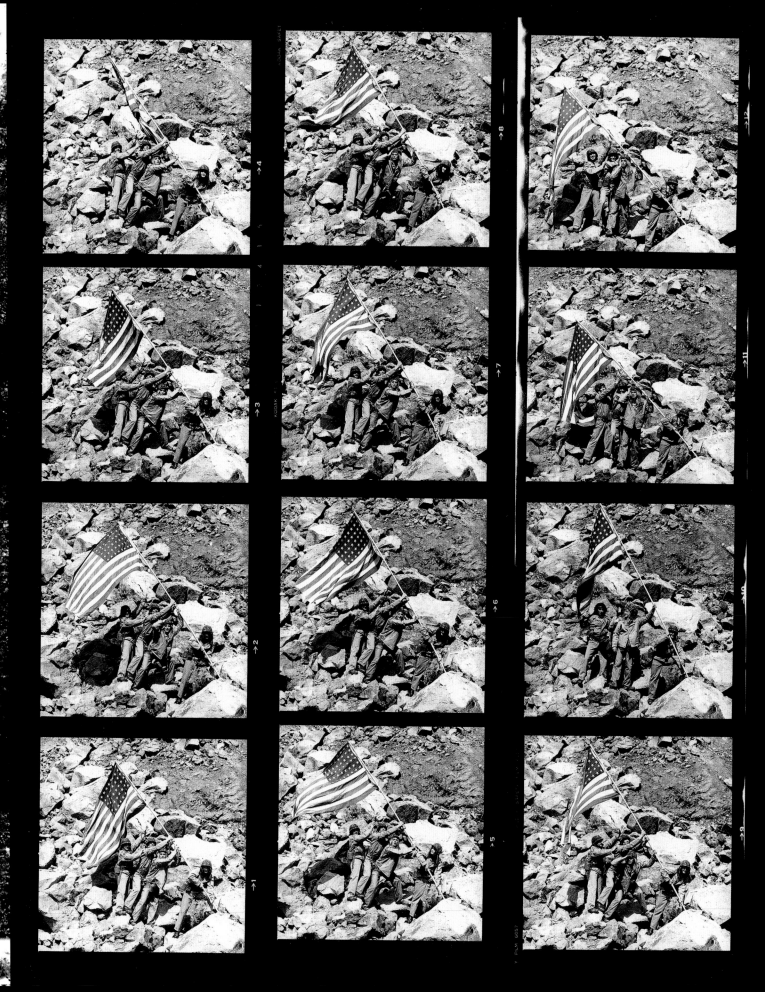

Van Halen is American Rock 'n' Roll. When we were in Hollywood cutting our second album in 1983, I ran into David Lee Roth at the Troubadour, surrounded by a bevy of slammin' babes and holding court like the star that he is. "Someday . . ." I thought. "Someday that will be us." Van Halen gave all of us something to strive for: the pure sonic rock that they defined. And the babe thing wasn't bad either.

— Jack Blades

The year was 1983 and the VH boys were scheduled to headline a three-day festival in Devore, California, called the US Festival. This concert was the BIGGEST / BADDEST rock 'n' roll show to be put on since Woodstock, and to show their power and dominance the VH boys came up with the brilliant idea to replicate the photograph of the marines at Iwo Jima raising the American flag after they conquered the Japanese.

We originally set out to do the photo about seven blocks from my studio in Hollywood, alongside of the 101 freeway in the side of a hill by the John Anson Ford Theater, and shot about two rolls of film. The problem was that when we looked at the Polaroids, we thought that the camouflage uniforms blended too much into the side of the mountain, so we had to find another location. We finally ended up on Forest Lawn Drive, right across from the Forest Lawn Mortuary and Mount Sinai Mortuary, next to the 134 freeway, and I took a very low angle with my camera so there would be nothing but sky behind them. We shot about two rolls of film and we nailed the picture perfectly!!!!!

— Neil Zlozower

In 1983 at the US Festival I watched what I thought at the time was the greatest rock band in the world. Van Halen. There wasn't anything they did that didn't make my jaw drop during their whole set. This was a real turning point in my view as a manager.

— Doc McGhee

The first time I heard "Eruption" I thought, "I HAVE to learn that!" Eddie was a HUGE influence on me and my playing. Of course, I had to buy a Kramer guitar, use white and black tape, and make my own Eddie-style guitar. Every Van Halen song I hear takes me to a different place or brings up old memories. It doesn't matter what mood you are in, throw in a Van Halen CD and it's gonna make ya wanna go through a wall. For guitar players, it makes you wanna learn something new. Eddie started a huge guitar revolution.

— Nick Catanese

Van Halen's first record was the first post-KISS-era band to really get me inspired. I felt like, "Hey, I can actually do that." It opened my eyes to what a great rock band could really be because everyone in the band was killer in their own way and had their own cool vibe. In fact, they inspired me to move to Los Angeles in 1983, which would become the impetus for my professional music career. Incidentally, playing the "Runnin' with the Devil" bass line early one morning from my apartment in Hollywood turned out to be an odd sort of audition for my next bass gig!

— David Ellefson

Last summer on tour, I got pulled up on Hatebreed's bus to watch a Van Halen video. It pretty much changed my life. David Lee Roth forgot the words and still outperformed most modern frontmen. Eddie played like he knew he was gonna be fucking your girlfriend later that night. Needless to say, I was sold.

— Zacky Vengeance

I was David Lee Roth for Halloween a few years ago and I will be him again probably this year too. Why? Because he is my idol. Since I was about five years old, I've recognized him as the God of Hard Rock, and he will not be topped. He is the quintessential bleach-blond California macho ladies' man who will tear it up onstage in pink assless chaps and show everyone how it's done. Bar none, the tops.

— Allison Robertson

When the band first decided to shoot the video for "Jump," there were a lot of scenes that were shot around Pasadena and Los Angeles that were supposed to be in the video. Then they went to a soundstage and shot the live performance footage. When the band looked at the performance footage, they thought it was SO STRONG that they decided to use the whole live shoot for the video, and then later used a lot of the L.A. and Pasadena footage for the "Panama" video.

— Neil Zlozower

I love Van Halen.
There is no mystery to why
they were successful.

– Alice Cooper

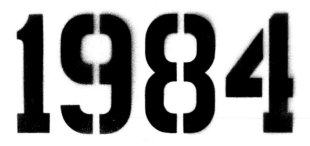

Thank God for engineer Donn Landee, who was always at my side knowing what I wanted and making great suggestions. "Jump" was recorded at Ed's studio. Donn and Ed put the track down alone in the middle of the night. We recut it once in one take for sonic reasons. Dave wrote the lyrics that afternoon in the backseat of his Mercury convertible. We finished all vocals that afternoon and mixed it that evening.

Everyone knows Ed's a genius, but few realize Dave is too. His lyrics are so beautifully abstract it's stunning. I tried to help him avoid the clichés we needed for hits. I learned a lot from them.

— Ted Templeman

When I was in my early twenties I was an unknown drummer touring the South with a guitar player named Gregg Wright. I was walking through a park in Baton Rouge and saw David Lee Roth sitting there with his bodyguard. I walked up and introduced myself. He was cool and gave me backstage passes to the show that night. It was the *1984* tour. It was an amazing show. When I went to try and say thanks I couldn't get near him. There were at least fifty girls standing in line waiting to see him. I knew I didn't stand a chance.

— Matt Sorum

Bigger-than-life sound. Bigger-than-life style. Van Halen had it all: talent, creativity, and an extremely vast body of work. They were truly unmatched, especially up through 1984. They could do it all. From "Runnin' with the Devil" to "Panama," they crushed the rock 'n' roll stereotype and rewrote the book. There can only be one.

— Craig Nunenmacher

When I was just a little boy, my mom would sit me down in front of the TV and all I wanted to watch was Van Halen. My mom knew that meant she had to turn on MTV because that's where we could watch Van Halen videos. I was obsessed. I even had my mom sign me up for the official fan club, where I received a signed poster by the band that I still have to this day.

— M. Shadows

Listening to those Van Halen records totally changed everything for me. There's no question their music was the soundtrack for my life. When I was nine I got *Van Halen I* because I was such a KISS fanatic that when I saw that Gene Simmons' name was listed in the Special Thanks section, I thought he was in the band without his makeup. I put on "Runnin' with the Devil" and "Eruption" and was totally blown away. I slowly started to put my KISS records away and became a fan, but was too young to go to the concerts. I had to wait until 1984, but once I saw the magic between Dave and Eddie on stage and the huge production, I knew I wanted to be Eddie Van Halen! I made a pact with myself: I wanted to play with David Lee Roth. Years later, in 1998, I got the chance and co-wrote most of his *DLR Band* record. A big thrill was hearing Eddie Van Halen say on a Detroit radio station that "Dave should stick with this guy."

— John 5

I still think that the main riff to "Ain't Talkin' 'Bout Love" is one of the coolest riffs ever written. To this day that's always the first thing I play when I grab a new guitar.

— Shavo Odadjian

213

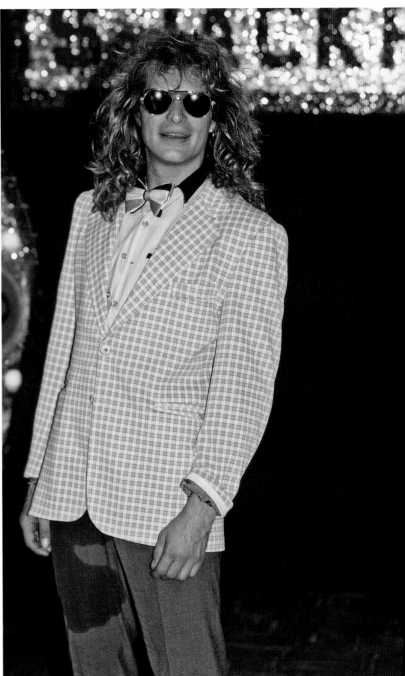

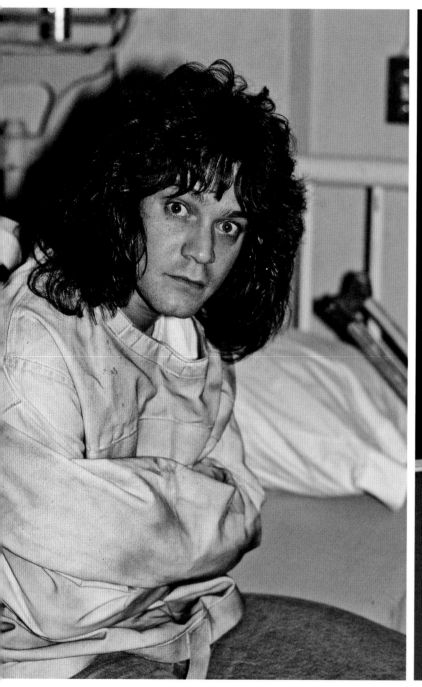

We were in Jacksonville, Florida, for the tour kickoff. At that time the country was having MICHAEL JACKSON fever and Michael could do no wrong. He was plastered all over the TV, newspapers and press. The night before the gig, we were all watching some awards show and Michael swept all the major awards. The next morning my phone rings at 6:30 A.M. and it's Dave waking me up, saying, "Hey Zloz! I want to do a photo shoot." I say in my half-asleep voice, "OK, MAN. When?" Dave says, "RIGHT NOW!" So, I go down to his room and he's all ready to shoot EXCEPT he's got his hair styled like Michael Jackson did on the awards show the night before. I thought Dave looked fucking COOL! So we shot a few rolls and then I went up to my room and back to sleep.

— Neil Zlozower

Van Halen were a rockin' band in the late '70s. At the time hard rock/metal bands had lots of male fans. Van Halen with their great sexy songs and image brought many females into the rock/metal scene. They had killer grooves and sounds, they jammed, and they all put on an amazing live show. Alex was and is a great rock drummer! I had a band with Dave for a minute. We had a rehearsal to check out a guitarist. Dave showed up in an outfit that looked to me like pajamas. So I said, "Hey Dave, are those your PJs?" He said, "No dude, I had these made special from a Holiday Inn curtain-bedspread set. These were custom made for me." I said, "They still look like pajamas." I never heard from him about the band again.

— Carmine Appice

At key points in history, events always seem to happen to advance the human story. The first time prehistoric man created tools. The invention of the light bulb, penicillin, the automobile, radio, TV, the Internet, etc. Van Halen was another such event. In the words of Winston Churchill, "Never was so much owed by so many to so few."

— Vito Bratta

I first heard Van Halen on the radio at a party in college, and it sounded like electric adrenaline. When this sonic elixir hit the country, it unleashed hard rock hysteria. At that time, the identity of most drummers was buried in triggers and reverb. But when you heard Alex, his sound and energy were undeniable, and the tone quality of Michael Anthony's background singing was also a distinctive stamp on the band's overall vibe.

Edward's contribution to rock guitar is immeasurable. It is only the most elite of elite musicians whose unconventional approach becomes convention. Some people are so utterly original that they can do only what comes naturally to them. Although Edward's technique shattered prevailing standards, it was his choice of notes and the way he phrased them that were the auditory expression of his personality. And that personality was enchanting on many levels.

David Lee Roth had a fiercely confident persona. He oozed chutzpah and eroticism. Those were the things that defined him as an entertainer, and they were the things his audiences lusted after. It always amused me to see pseudo rock stars of the time feverishly attempting to copy his brilliance. Remember all those half-assed airborne leg splits to some watered-down, cookie-cutter version of "Panama"? Those novices never truly understood the self-discipline and focused vision Dave had in achieving his goals. He was underailable and intense, very intense. Did I mention he was intense?

Music fans often speculate about what the band might be like today if it hadn't gone through so many breakups. Who knows? Maybe they'd be selling out the entire Sahara Desert by now. But if Dave had always stayed in the band, I would never have had the chance to join his solo group. And I would never have gotten to Eat 'Em and Smile.

— Steve Vai

He brought tapping to the forefront, and I still think he was one of the tastiest players doing it. It wasn't his fault that all these other horrendous people tried to emulate him. I actually saw Eddie play some blues once and it was really beautiful. It would be great to hear him play more in that style.

— Jeff Beck

The way many guys of my generation would look at *Star Wars* as their fondest childhood obsession is how I usually describe the long-lasting effect Van Halen has had on me. I play electric guitar for a living now, and I consider that fact largely due to Eddie. The first time I saw Eddie Van Halen walk atop the desks playing the "Hot for Teacher" solo I was like, "Why are both of his hands on the neck? That's what I wanna do!" But it wasn't just Eddie, it was the band's intensity and musicality as a unit, it was their showmanship, their sense of humor, so many great songs and their live energy, which I would compare to some kind of before-its-time extreme sport. For the first few years that I played guitar, Van Halen records were the only thing I would listen to. As of late, I have a Van Halen shrine in my house. I've done college projects about them. There were Van Halen records playing at my wedding. They are my *Star Wars* and I grew up on Planet Tatooine.

— Fred Mascherino

When it really comes down to it, the sound of Edward's guitar is what makes Van Halen instantly recognizable. They emerged in an era when rock groups had to create their own unique sound to be noticed by major labels. The sound of Edward's guitar combined with Alex's drums on the original records was positively brobdingnagian. It melted your speakers and it made you wonder how it was possible to do what they were doing. They had great songs with great arrangements, and David Lee Roth was the perfect extra ingredient to put things over the top. When they hit the stage in their heyday they were untouchable. Not only were they serious motherfuckers when it came to playing, but they put on a show that was as uplifting as it was awe inspiring. You walked away from one of their concerts energized.

— Dweezil Zappa

Eddie Van Halen invented metal guitar, plain and simple. It wasn't done before, there was no conception of this complex art prior to his existence, and to top it off, if his metal chops weren't enough to boggle minds for the next few decades, he threw in his right hand to help his left tackle the most eccentric, yet extremely tasteful, fingerboard schemes to date. Metal is the prophetic son and brainchild of Eddie Van Halen.

— Syn Gates

It was December of '06 and my wife and I were out cruisin' around listening to satellite radio with our three-year-old in the backseat when Van Halen's "You Really Got Me" started ripping out of the car speakers. When it got to the guitar solo my son asked if he would need two guitar picks to play like that! Nearly three decades later and even a three-year-old knows that Eddie's guitar playing ain't from this fucking planet!

— Tom Keifer

I remember standing on my chair at Long Beach Arena seeing Van Halen just rip shit! They were the coolest thing I had seen. Two years later I shared the same stage with them on the Monsters of Rock tour in Europe. Wow! Life is crazy!!!

— Tommy Lee

Alex and Eddie are the dynamic duo of music. Not only are they great songwriters, but incredible musicians. Alex was a big influence on me when I started playing drums.

— Raymond I. Herrera

If it wasn't for Alex I'd still be wondering what in the hell to do with a pair of drumsticks in a rock 'n' roll song.

— Rikki Rockett

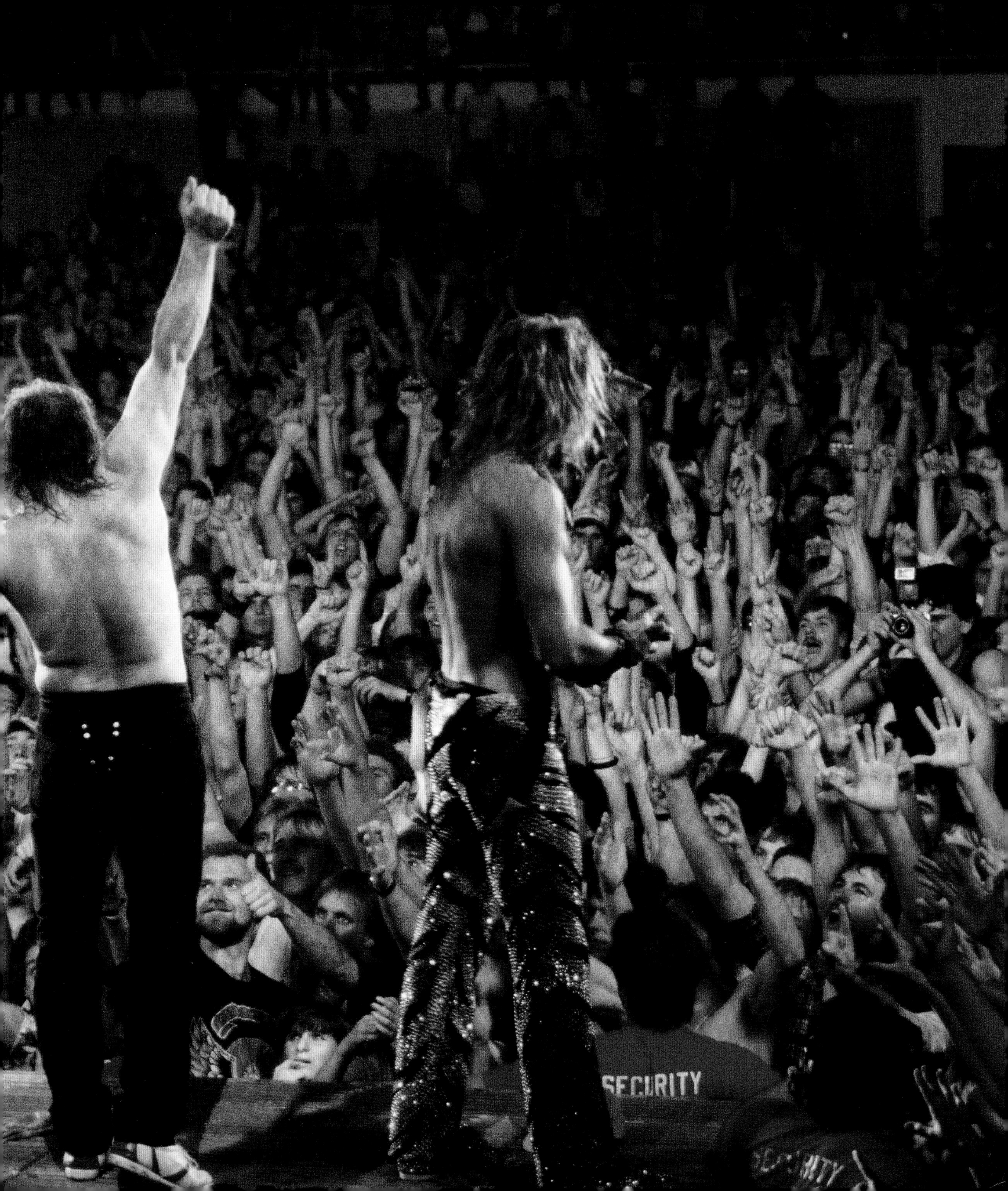
SECURITY

Contributors (In alphabetical order)

Joey Allen (guitarist: Warrant)
Eddie Anderson (director of security 1980–84)
Pete Angelus (creative consultant, production / lighting designer)
Michael Anthony (bassist)
Carmine Appice (drummer)
Vinny Appice (drummer)
Jeff Beck (guitarist)
Burton C. Bell (singer: Fear Factory)
Charlie Benante (drummer: Anthrax)
Marshall Berle (personal manager 1977–79)
Rodney Bingenheimer (legendary Los Angeles DJ)
Jack Blades (singer/bassist: Night Ranger, Damn Yankees, Shaw/Blades)
Vito Bratta (guitarist: White Lion)
Vivian Campbell (guitarist: Def Leppard)
Nick Catanese (guitarist: Black Label Society)
Phil Collen (guitarist: Def Leppard)
Alice Cooper (singer)
Fred Coury (drummer: Cinderella)
David Coverdale (singer: Whitesnake)
M. Shawn Crahan (percussionist: Slipknot)
Juan Croucier (bassist: Ratt)
Craig DeFalco (guitarist: Laidlaw)
Jimmy DeGrasso (drummer: Megadeth, David Lee Roth)
Warren DeMartini (guitarist: Ratt)
Ronnie James Dio (singer: DIO, Black Sabbath)
Don Dokken (singer: Dokken)
Elliot Easton (guitarist: The Cars)
Blas Elias (drummer: Slaughter)
David Ellefson (bassist: Megadeth)
Joe Elliott (singer: Def Leppard)
John 5 (guitarist: Rob Zombie, Marilyn Manson, David Lee Roth)
Mark Friedman (music publisher: Chrysalis Music)
Syn Gates (guitarist: Avenged Sevenfold)
Billy Gibbons (guitarist: ZZ Top)
Paul Gilbert (guitarist: Mr. Big, Racer X)
Ross Halfin (photographer)
Rob Halford (singer: Judas Priest)
Raymond I. Herrera (drummer: Fear Factory)
Scott Ian (guitarist: Anthrax)
Grover Jackson (founder: Jackson Guitars)
Joey Jordison (drummer: Slipknot)
Tom Keifer (singer/guitarist: Cinderella)
Kerry King (guitarist: Slayer)
Bruce Kulick (guitarist: Grand Funk Railroad, KISS)
Tommy Lee (drummer: Mötley Crüe)

Lemmy (singer/bassist: Motörhead)
Steve Lukather (guitarist: Toto)
Mick Mars (guitarist: Mötley Crüe)
Fred Mascherino (guitarist: Taking Back Sunday)
Miljenko Matijevic (singer: SteelHeart)
Doc McGhee (legendary manager: KISS, Bon Jovi, Mötley Crüe)
Tom Morello (guitarist: Rage Against The Machine, Audioslave)
Rick Nielsen (guitarist: Cheap Trick)
Ted Nugent (guitarist/singer)
Craig Nunenmacher (drummer: Black Label Society)
Shavo Odadjian (bassist: System Of A Down)
Jimmy Page (guitarist: Led Zeppelin)
Les Paul (guitarist, Gibson Les Paul designer, and inventor)
Vinnie Paul (drummer: Pantera, Hellyeah)
Stephen Pearcy (singer: Ratt)
Allison Robertson (guitarist: The Donnas)
Rikki Rockett (drummer: Poison)
Henry Rollins (singer)
James Root (guitarist: Slipknot, Stone Sour)
David Lee Roth (singer: Van Halen)
Joe Satriani (guitarist)
Rick Savage (bassist: Def Leppard)
M. Shadows (singer: Avenged Sevenfold)
Billy Sheehan (bassist: David Lee Roth, Talas)
Gene Simmons (singer/bassist: KISS)
Eric Singer (drummer: KISS, Alice Cooper, Badlands)
Nikki Sixx (bassist: Mötley Crüe)
Slash (guitarist: Velvet Revolver, Guns N' Roses)
Chad Smith (drummer: Red Hot Chili Peppers)
Matt Sorum (drummer: Velvet Revolver, Guns N' Roses)
Paul Stanley (singer/guitarist: KISS)
Steve Stevens (guitarist: Billy Idol)
Jaime St. James (singer: Warrant, Black 'N Blue)
Ted Templeman (producer)
Tommy Thayer (guitarist: KISS, Black 'N Blue)
Brad Tolinski (editor-in-chief: *Guitar World* magazine)
Mike Tramp (singer: White Lion)
Erik Turner (guitarist: Warrant)
Steve Vai (guitarist: David Lee Roth, Frank Zappa)
Zacky Vengeance (guitarist: Avenged Sevenfold)
Brad Wilk (drummer: Rage Against The Machine, Audioslave)
Kip Winger (singer/bassist: Winger)
Zakk Wylde (guitarist: Ozzy Osbourne, Black Label Society)
Dweezil Zappa (guitarist)